SOCIAL MEDIA MARKETING
For Business Domination

I0467660

David Odunaiya
&
Abiola Fashina Esq

Table of Contents

INTRODUCTION

Social media marketing is an incredibly powerful tool and these days it is one of the single biggest factors that a marketer can use to build their digital empire. In fact, social media is often what really makes the difference between having a website and having such an 'empire'.

A website on its own can make you money and it can promote your business – but it takes more than that to build a brand and to have that ubiquitous presence that can help you to drive the maximum amount of traffic to your monetization systems.

Social media allows you to interact with your audience, to get feedback, to hear suggestions and to communicate in a variety of different ways. It lets you build brand visibility and it lets you drive visitors directly to your site. This is why social media is so important and it is why so many people and businesses are hopping on board In fact,

How Social Media Goes Wrong

A lot of businesses and even dedicated social media marketers are under the impression that they can just set up an account and post regularly with the hopes that they will start generating lots of followers and 'likes'. There is no planning and no foresight and there is no attempt to take full advantage of the more advanced features and uses.

What is worse is that many of these companies use social media sites simply as a place to advertise. All they are doing is posting and all they are posting is things like 'Our web design service is the best in the business!'

Think honestly, is this an account you would follow yourself? Are any of these posts things you would potentially share with other users? If not, then you cannot really expect your channel to grow. The result is something pitiful – a completely empty social media channel with you mentioning the merits of your business to an empty room and pretending someone is listening. This can actually be more damaging to your brand than not having a social media account at all!

In addition, this is hardly what you would call 'building a digital empire'. So with that in mind, let us look at how you should be approaching your social media efforts and at how you can make it really work for you.

What You Will Learn

By the end of this book, you will know how to:
- Create a consistent and engaging brand across social media
- Use social media for much more than just brand awareness
- Set up accounts with all the major social media accounts
- Build a rapport with your visitors and gain their trust

- Provide engaging content that people want to read and share
- Set up tools to automate a lot of the work and save you time
- Create synergy between your social media channels to drive more traffic and grow faster
- Use growth hacking to get even more traffic to your accounts
- Run competitions and other events to get more traffic
- Leverage events and competitions.

And more

Chapter One

Social Media Does More Than Build Brand Awareness.

The first thing to recognize about your social media efforts is that your objectives should go beyond simply getting more people to follow you and to see your brand. Social media is ideal for strengthening brand awareness but it is also a tool that can be used in many other ways. Here are just some of the things you can do once you have learned to master your social media presence...

Get Feedback and Survey Your Audience

Companies will often pay a lot of money to conduct surveys and to interview their audience. Using social media though, you can do exactly that and can thereby hone your products and services to get the best possible feedback.

You can also get a lot of rich data by looking at how your social media is performing. For instance, which titles are getting clicked on the most often? What type of images illicit sharing?

Networking and Influencer Marketing

Originally, most social networks were not designed to be

David Odunaiya & Abiola Fashina Esq.

platforms for marketing. Rather, they were intended to facilitate networking so that people could find like-minded individuals and potentially business contacts in the case of sites like LinkedIn.

This is something you can use social media for in a very effective manner and potentially it can be highly powerful once you do.

They say that success is about whom you know and with social media you have means of reaching people you otherwise would struggle to. Particularly with LinkedIn, you can this way get in touch with 'influencers', who are individuals in your niche or industry that hold great sway and who can act as a bridge to help you reach a huge audience. Using influencer marketing, it is often possible to go from just a couple of followers to thousands overnight.

Likewise, social media can be used to find clients, business contacts and more.

Contact Management

In some ways, you can consider social media to be a contact management tool. You can easily use sites like Google+ and LinkedIn to categorize and organize your contacts and then to easily get in touch with them when you need to discuss something. Using the same tool to find your contacts as you do to organize and contact them has a large number of advantages.

In-House Communication

You can also use social media marketing for direct communication within your team. Creating groups, pages and events lets you discuss things with your team and work on collaborative projects while keeping everything in the same place. Some tools are at once social networks and project management applications, which has a great number of advantages.

Leads and Direct Sales

You can of course use social media to generate leads and to build a mailing list but you can also use it to directly generate sales. Through advertising or well-constructed posts with an embedded link, you can send followers straight to a checkout and in some cases even have them buy directly through the social network.

For affiliate marketers, it is incredibly easy to start making money from Facebook. All they need to do is to create a landing page to sell an affiliate product (meaning they make commission), then set up a 'PPC' (pay per click) advertising campaign on Facebook. Now the campaign will generate visitors who will instantly convert into customers and if this has been set up well, then it will create more profit than it costs.

Enhancing Your Service

Social media also has benefits for your customers and can be used to improve the experience of using your business. Whether you use follow up questions, or just provide your users with a way to get in touch, this can add an extra dimension to their experience and help to improve their experience.

These are some examples of how social networks can be used as more than just a means to improve brand visibility. There are many more uses for social media beyond this though, so ensure that you take the time to explore your options and to find unique ways to use social media in your own business.

Chapter 2

Best Practices for Social Networking

Now you know what social networking can be used for, the next thing to start looking at is how precisely you are going to use it.

Of course, each social network is different and the best strategy to use on Twitter will be different from the strategy to use on Facebook. Nevertheless, there are some hard and fast rules that apply across the board and the overall strategy will often be the same. Read on then and we will look at how you can start building that digital empire through social media...

Setting Up – 'Be Everywhere'

Before you can do anything else, you will first need to set up your social media accounts and begin building connections between them. Getting this right at the start will save you a lot of time and it is ultimately what's necessary to ensure you get the most from your efforts.

What's key is that you create a strong brand that will be memorable and recognizable. From there, you are then going to take that branding and spread it across social media, thereby creating as many opportunities for potential leads to discover you as possible and at the same time reinforcing the connection your audience has with your company.

This is important because eventually you are going to link all of your disparate social media accounts and it is important that the transition be smooth when a visitor goes from one to the other. This needs to feel like a continuous experience, as though they are going from one room to another in the same building. If you do not manage this, then rather than strengthening your brand, the multiple accounts will only create confusion.

Having a consistent presence across your different accounts feels professional, it impresses users and it helps them to remember that they are dealing with your business. Essentially, you're trying to make your Twitter and Facebook accounts look as much like your website as you possibly can using the tools that you've been given.

So how do you create a consistent image and branding? Your company name is part of your brand of course but also important is to ensure you have a specific design language. This should come through in your logo but also in your cover image and in the color scheme and pictures, you choose for your social media pages. This same language should also be present on your website.

Now you need to repeat this process on as many different social accounts as you can. We have addressed a number of social networks specifically in this book, so make sure that you are at least present on each of these:

- Facebook
- Twitter
- Pinterest

- Instagram
- Google+
- LinkedIn
- YouTube

Each of these is another opportunity for your people to find you and it provides a link back to your website which will act like the 'hub' of your network. Each will offer a different aspect of your business but all of them will remain on message and consistently designed.

At the same time, your website should be linked back to all of these accounts. This way, visitors to your site can decide how they would like to keep up-to-date with what you're doing and they can click the relevant link to do so. A simple 'Like Us on Facebook' banner can help your business to grow as your website feeds your Facebook account and vice versa.

Using Tools to Automate Your Social Media

Being on lots of different accounts at once might sound like a lot of work but the good news is that you will not have to handle all these different channels manually. Thankfully, there are countless tools available that are designed to streamline the process of maintaining a strong social media presence and these include numerous things that can link together your accounts or that can auto-generate content.

Something important to keep in mind is that a 'dead' social media account is actually worse than having none at all. You do not want it to look like you have forgotten about your Facebook page, or your Twitter account, so you need to keep updating regularly – and these tools can help you to do that.

Here are some examples:

Buffer

Buffer (www.bufferapp.com) is a very simple web app that allows you to schedule your posts for some of the major search engines. This then means that you can then write thousands of words for Twitter and have them posted over a set period of time at regular intervals. In turn, this means that your account won't look empty even when you haven't had a good opportunity to post anything new.

Hootsuite

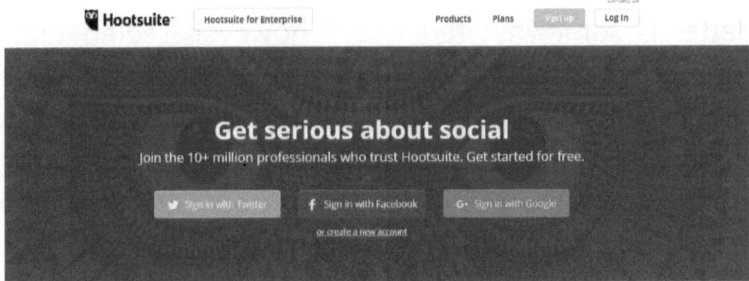

Hootsuite (www.hootsuite.com) is a handy tool that does what Buffer does and more. As well as being able to schedule posts, Hootsuite will let you view multiple feeds from different social networks at once (so you can be fully updated all in one place) and it lets you post to multiple places at once.

IFTTT (www.ifttt.com)

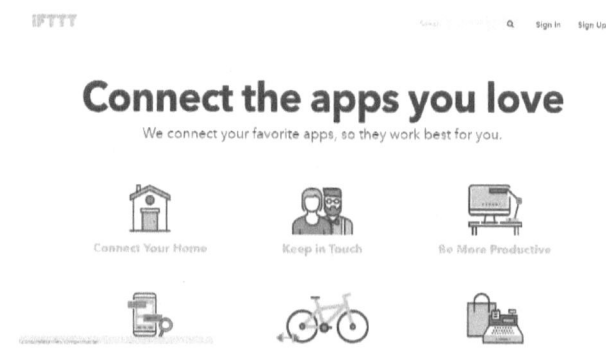

IFTTT stands for 'If This, Then That' and allows you to set up relationships between different apps you're using, your mobile phone and even some hardware. This means you could have your Nest thermostat Tweet about the temperature you have set up in your house, or it means you could have Facebook posts automatically shared to Twitter.

The latter is somewhat redundant however, seeing that you can use features built into most social networks and even WordPress and YouTube to cross pollinate your accounts these days. Nevertheless, for advanced rules and even auto-generated posts there is a lot be gained here and it's very much worth taking a look and applying some though.

Providing Value

Now you are everywhere, it is important to make sure that people view this as a good thing rather than a bad thing. In other words, being everywhere does not automatically mean that people are going to start following you or that they are going to enjoy your content. More important than creating your accounts and linking them is providing value through them and filling them with engaging content.

We have already discussed the mistake that some users will make – to set up a social media account and then simply post about how good their product is. This is not going to get people to follow you and it certainly will not lead to more shares.

On the other hand, though, if you Tweet or post something funny, interesting or useful then someone might actually follow you and they may even share what you have written. In terms of status updates and Tweets, you provide value by letting people learn about the industry you are in, by inspiring them, by offering discounts and by providing entertainment.

A lot of companies worry that it will be 'unprofessional' to discuss anything other than their own services but this then leads to them lacking any interest, personality or bite. Instead, post about the industry, post tips on how to get more out of your products and make comments relating to the lifestyle that you are trying to promote.

That last one is important by the way: the 'lifestyle' aspect is what gives your product or service its emotional hook and it is what will enable you to make your business into more of a 'movement' rather than just another corporation.

If you sell fitness equipment, then you should be talking about the trials of the gym and posting pictures of attractive people running on the beach with their muscles rippling.

People who enjoy the fitness lifestyle love this kind of content. On the other hand, if you provide a premium B2B service, then talk business tips and stock market and post pictures of people looking productive wearing suits and looking out of high rise buildings.

Now you are providing value, entertainment and information and you are giving your audience something to actual engage with. Just make sure that you maintain your consistent image by staying on message and by sticking to the topic – fluctuating all over, the place with your subject matter is a big mistake.

Articles and Blog Posts

As well as status updates and pictures, most social networks will also let you post links to articles and blogs. This is arguably even more important when it comes to providing value, engaging with the audience and getting likes and shares. There is only so much value you can provide in a few hundred characters but with an article, you can deliver something that is really worth reading and thus worth sharing and potentially evens subscribing too.

There are two ways; you can provide this type of content. The first way – and the best way – is to create your own content on a blog. This way you can keep people engaged with your brand while at the same time strengthening your authority and building trust. You can demonstrate yourself to be an expert in other words, thereby creating a situation where your visitors will likely start seeking you out intentionally to get your opinion (which means you will be able to market to them easily).

According to Social Media Examiner, blogging is the most important area that 68% of marketers plan to focus on in the coming years. Blogging is also, what can tie together your search engine optimization, your social media and your website into a single package. This is called 'content marketing' and it is a very important thing to consider.

We will be looking at how to create great content that people will want to read and share later when we get to the Facebook chapter. For now, just know that you need to be creating and finding amazing, interesting, entertaining and unique content for your website. Likewise, make sure you add social sharing buttons such as those from Shareaholic (www.shareaholic.com). This way, your visitors will be able to easily take the initiative and share your content with the rest of the web and across their own social networks.

Chapter 3

Twitter

We have looked at how to set up social media networks, we have seen how they can be used and we have looked at how to provide value. Now it is time to get down to the nitty gritty and to see how best to approach each of the big social media sites.

We will start with Twitter. Twitter has long been one of the largest and best known social networks on the web and it has a very special set of advantages for big businesses.

The main appeal of Twitter is that it is low investment, high yield. In other words, it will take you a couple of seconds to Tweet something but that Tweet could potentially be seen by thousands or even millions of people.

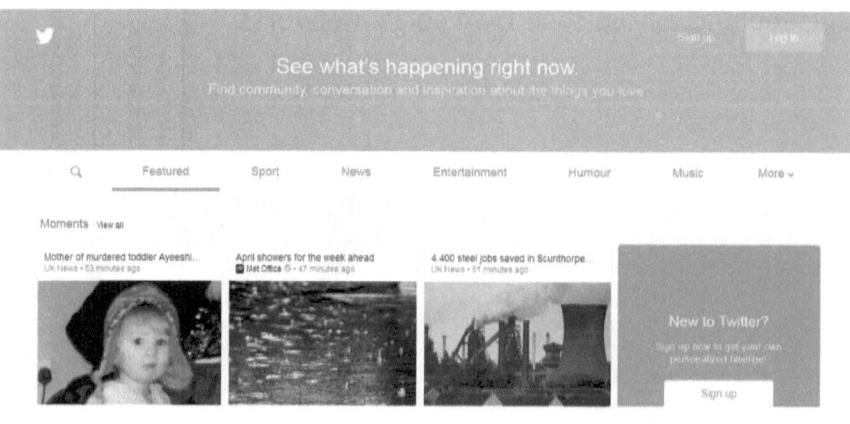

How Twitter Works

The way that Twitter works is simple. This network allows you to post a Tweet of 140 characters to your audience, which should normally reflect your opinion on a matter, your mood, or an interesting idea, fact or tip. Everyone who is one of your 'followers' will then see that Tweet. At the same time, other people will also be able to search for the Tweet by searching for phrases you used within the message, or by searching for 'hashtags'.

Essentially a hashtag is something that allows you to tag the subject matter of your post and thus helps people to find posts on that subject. The great thing about hashtags is that specific phrases can end up 'trending' which can then provide huge exposure for Tweets on that subject.

Likewise, popular Tweets can also be favorited by other users, or 'Retweeted' (shared) with their audience.

Generally, the idea behind Twitter is that it gives you a quick way to see what people are talking about and to join the discussion. By searching for a specific tag, you can see how people on Twitter are responding to that event and you can even get breaking news this way. Twitter itself has gone so far as to describe the platform as the 'pulse of the planet'.

How to Succeed on Twitter

Twitter has a very specific 'vibe' to it and a hip, youthful reputation. Succeeding here often means being somewhat candid and personable, with bland corporate messages sinking into obscurity.

If you run a small business, then this is a great place to Tweet about how the 'office is quiet this morning' or how you are 'super excited to be working on X new project'. You can get more personal if you have a personal brand and for instance use this to talk about how you are feeling. The idea is that fans will get a glimpse into your life and your lifestyle.

Guy Kawasaki knows how to "enchant" his audience

Another way to demonstrate that your company is modern and in-style is to look at what is happening right now and to join the discussion. Keep your eyes on the news and look for trending subjects and then chime in – this way; you'll be able to get a lot of eyes on your posts just by riding the wave. Tweet about something that is currently being discussed and as long as it is not so big that your message gets drowned, then you can gain a lot of followers and Retweets this way.

Of course, the best kind of news for a business is breaking news in their industry. So make sure that you post this type of content. Getting hash tags right is really the secret to success here and to rapid growth.

You can also provide bite-sized tips on Twitter and bits of information. Users say they also like to follow brands that share special offers and discounts with their audience – which of course has an inherent value for your audience.

Tools and Tips to Grow Your Audience Quickly and Effectively

To take your efforts on Twitter even further, you should also look at employing some tools and techniques in smart ways.

We have already seen how Buffer can be useful to create lots of Tweets that will then be delivered over time. This is a good strategy but do make sure that you are writing fresh content too – you cannot react to current events and trending topics if everything you post is automated!

Another key strategy for growth on Twitter is to engage with your most influential followers. If you can get someone with 2,000 followers to Retweet your comment, then that means you will have just gotten exposure to 2,000 more people in moments. To do this, you can use Twitter's in-built analytics feature to see which of your users are the biggest and most influential (www.analytics.twitter.com). From there, you can then target those 'best' followers by responding to their tweets, by sharing things they say and generally by engaging with them. If you share one of their tweets, then often they will reciprocate and do the same.

A tip though: don't try and aim too high right from the start. If you go for a Twitter user with 100,000,000 followers, then they will likely ignore you – they get a billion messages a day after all. Instead, look for users that have lots of followers but aren't 'out of your league'. Likewise, using tools like Twitter Analytics and Followerwonk (www.followerwonk.com) you can also see which of your users is already engaging with lots of your content. Find someone who is engaged and influential and you have your perfect storm!

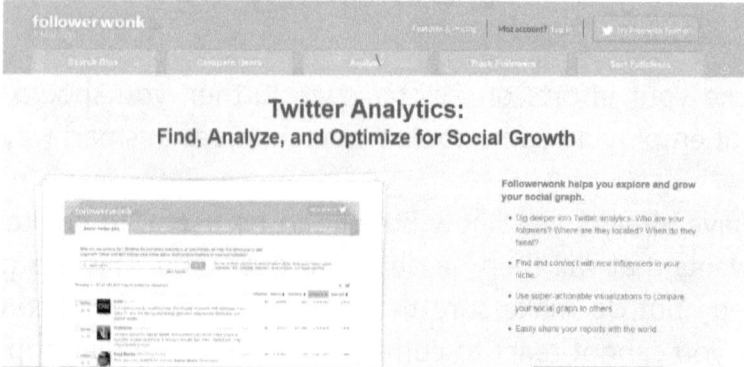

Follower Wonk will give you useful analytics

This tool also lets you see when your followers are most active – very handy for knowing when to schedule your tweets.

Chapter 4

Pinterest

Pinterest is tool that too many businesses and users are overlooking. Pinterest does not have quite the same reputation as Facebook and Twitter but it is expected to hit 50 million active users in the US alone by 2016. That is not a small number and it is worth taking notice of.

Some brands are doing very big numbers on Pinterest too: Etsy has over 461,000 followers, while Swarovski's 'Wedded Bliss' board has an incredible 1,537,213 subscribers.

What's more, Pinterest is somewhat different from some of the other social networks on this list. For instance, it has a large proportion of female users (71%) which is excellent if that is your target demographic or if it is a demographic, you have been struggling to crack.

How Pinterest Works

First, it is pertinent to examine precisely how Pinterest works and how it is different from another social network like Twitter. Essentially, Pinterest lets users create mood boards (just called 'boards' on Pinterest). They do this by pinning content they find either online, or content that they find by browsing other boards. The result is a collage of images that they have found,

collected in a single place and with optional added comments.

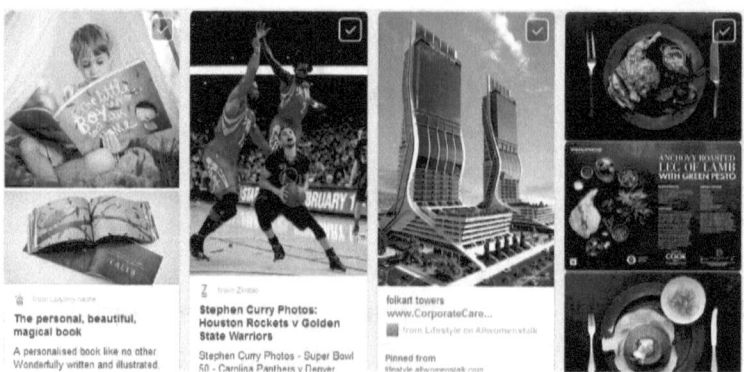

So what is a mood board for? Usually, it acts as a source of inspiration for a project, or perhaps a scrapbook of ideas and things that you like. So if you were about to plan a wedding for instance, you would likely sign up to Pinterest and start searching for wedding inspiration – decorations, venues, bridesmaid dresses, seating plans, table names, flowers etc. etc.

From here, you would then hopefully find inspiration for things you liked and you could then pin that to your own board. Eventually, you would start to come up with a visual direction for your wedding and you would have a ton of ideas all in one place. Other features include the ability to let other users edit your board (your partner or best man/maid of honor) or to make the board private. Of course, you can also upload your own images, which might include photos you have taken.

In your search for wedding inspiration, you might then find yourself following boards of other users that have provided you with lots of good ideas. And in fact, if you were to create your own board, you might find that some other users start following you too!

Succeeding on Pinterest

So that is the general principle, now how do you make it work for you and really start to succeed on Pinterest?

The first thing to recognize is that once again, the key to success is very much to provide value. Rather than providing 'general' value though, there is a specific type of value that does very well on Pinterest. The key is to remember why people use Pinterest in the first place, the answer to which is to find inspiration, to collect ideas and to create attractive and thought provoking boards.

As well as wedding planning, many users will use Pinterest to create motivational boards to help them stick to their gym routine, they will create boards for web design and they will create boards for fashion tips. They might meanwhile like following boards that offer these things, which provide fonts, which share cool images from films or comics, etc.

Thus, you need to find an 'angle' like this that will work within your niche or your industry. What is the lifestyle you are trying to promote? How can you sell that lifestyle through a board? Certain industries of course lend themselves to this type of content very well. If you own a crafts business for instance, or if you sell clothes, then there are some obvious ways, you can provide inspiration and ideas while at the same time subtly promoting your brand.

If you sell insurance though, then having a successful Pinterest board might be more difficult. The key here is again to look at the underlying lifestyle that goes with your offering. If you sell life insurance, then you might create Pinterest boards about family days out, things you can do together etc. If you sell home insurance, then you can create Pinterest boards of interior designs or beautiful homes.

These can gather their own momentum to the point where they are very successful independently from your business – giving you the perfect launch pad to then promote your products or services. For this to happen though you need to spend some real time with Pinterest and you need to treat it like its own product. Keep thinking: how can you make this board better? What new content might people want to see?

Finally, if you run a blog then in all likelihood you will be posting images alongside each new article (at least you should!). You can simply share these to Pinterest as well as a way for people to stay up to date with what you are doing.

More Tips to Accelerate Your Pinterest Success

Pinterest is a great tool for running campaigns, competitions and events. If you have a visual product like a line of clothes for instance, then you could challenge your followers to create their own pins and boards using them. You can then share the best ones in order to gain more momentum. This is a great way to generate some hype and some interaction with your followers and as an added bonus, you'll also be able to see how people are using the things you've created – which in turn might help you to come up with ideas for new features etc.

Also important of course is to ensure that you keep updating your Pinterest with new content. Creating new images can be hard work but if all you do is 'repin' pins from other boards, then you will not be contributing much new and there will not be much benefit for you when your own pins get shared. Really, your board should showcase your brand, your products and your industry in a unique way.

Fortunately, there is a plugin for Pinterest that is very helpful. Using this, you will see a pin icon in the top corner of any image when you hover your mouse over the top of it. This way, you can simply click that icon and then easily add the image to one of your boards. This is great for building a big collection of images on any board quickly.

Go to https://help.pinterest.com/en/articles/add-pinterest-browser-button to add a Pinterest button to your browser.

Chapter 5:
Facebook

Facebook remains the biggest social network of all. In fact, when many people think 'social network' they think Facebook. Facebook has so many users that if it were a country, it would be one of the largest in the world. There is a ton of opportunity here and there are countless different tools that can help you to get more from it.

Let us take a look at how success on Facebook works...

Facebook for Businesses

If you are going to try to succeed on Facebook, then the first thing you will need is a Facebook page. Unlike Twitter or other social networks, you do not just create an account for your business on Facebook but also rather use your personal account to set up a 'Page' that will then represent your business.

Your Facebook page though will look rather like a Facebook profile – with a profile and cover image. From there, you can then post status updates, pictures and links. When you post these things, it will be shared with the followers you have accrued. However, you will not reach 100% of those followers and instead will tend to reach about 16%. So if you have 100 followers, then everything you post will be seen by about 16 people each time.

Therefore, that is not very much... Facebook's argument for doing this is that the home feed was simply becoming too crowded for most people, though in reality it was likely also motivated by financial gain; paying to promote a Facebook post means that more of your followers will see it.

Either way, a canny post will often reach more than just the page's followers. That is because all of the same options and features exist for page posts as they do for other posts. So if someone were to comment on your post, then this might be seen by friends of that person. Likewise, people can share your posts with their own network, or they 'Like' them. Friends will also see when people like your page.

This then means that in theory, Facebook can facilitate a post going viral. If enough people see your link and share it, then it will proliferate throughout different social networks until millions of people have seen it.

One or two other features also exist on Facebook for businesses. For instance, you have the option to create a 'Call to Action' for your page, which means you can get people to sign up to your mailing list or to send an e-mail to you by clicking a button that lives at the top of the page.

Finally, there are Facebook ads which can work on a PPC basis (pay per click) or even a CPA basis (Cost Per Action). The latter is very interesting as it means you might only pay when someone downloads your free app, or when someone signs up to your mailing list.

How to Succeed on Facebook

The most popular and successful pages on Facebook are the ones that regularly share useful content from around the web – and particularly those that share content they created themselves. If you have a blog or a website, then this is the ideal place to share your content and to get many eyes on it.

To maximize the benefit from this though, your aim should be to create posts that will get clicked and that will get shared. To do this, you need to understand what type of content does well on Facebook.

And unfortunately, the main thing that should come to mind here is the infamous 'clickbait'. Clickbait is content with topics and with titles that have been specifically designed to get people to click it, without necessarily giving much regard to the quality that it provides. Sometimes the quality is there of course and the article will deliver on its promise. In other cases though, it is essentially amounts to a 'trap' for the reader.

What might a clickbait title look like? Often these will use curiosity in order to encourage people to click. For instance: "You'll never believe what happens at the end of this video... I nearly lost my mind!" In other cases the articles might be purposefully controversial, they might suggest some kind of gossip or they might make outrageous claims. Examples might be "This one trick can build pounds of muscle overnight. But should it be legal?" or "Executives at Apple are FURIOUS With Microsoft for this Latest Scandal'.

Other titles will promise incredible results: "How this drink can change your life forever – boosts brain power up to 500%!" Finally, some will combine several of these strategies in one title: "You'll never believe the strange way this young boy DOUBLED his brain power!" This same strategy will also often be used in adverts – like the '1 Weird Trick' you always hear about.

These titles work because people cannot help but be curious. Sure, it is probably nonsense but what if it is not? Does it really hurt to take a few seconds to click the link?

But while this method might work, that doesn't mean that you should be doing it yourself. Why? Because although you will get many visitors, you will also probably damage your reputation – and quite possibly irreparably. People do not like being tricked and if they feel that one of your articles has conned them, then they will be unlikely to want to click on another of your links in future.

So what do you do instead? Simple: you create links that are this unique, this interesting and this bombastic... but that actually deliver. And the main way to do that? That would be to come up with content that is actually completely original and that puts a new angle on a popular topic.

The problem with a lot of content on the web these days is that it is bland, derivative and done before. How many articles have you seen on 'how to get a six pack'? How often have you seen the 'Top 10 Healthiest Foods'? It is boring! But what you might not have heard of is 'cardio acceleration' – a cool sounding training method that can genuinely enhance fat burning (something like 135% according to actual research). Or what about an in-depth post on foods that boost mitochondrial function to increase energy levels to 'that of a young child'?

These topics elicit curiosity because most of us will not be familiar with things like cardio acceleration. It sounds cool and interesting and we can imagine what it might do but we need to read to find out. And when we do, we're not disappointed.

Your objective then should be to come up with content that is new. That means reading into your topic in depth, it means combining different related subjects and it means reading scientific research in many cases too.

Again the best litmus test is whether you would read it. Ask yourself: would that title be enough that you would just have to click it if you hadn't written it yourself? And would the content being delivered live up to your hopes once you did click it? Once you master that, you will find you start to get more people reading your content and more people choosing to follow your page.

Content That Gets Shared

That's how you write content that will get read. Now how do you create content that will get shared? Again, this comes down to understanding the psychology of social media. Why do people share the content they share?

And to figure this out, we need to remember that ultimately, social networks are communication tools. People share content primarily then as a way to communicate. That means they will either share content as a way to express themselves, or as a way to show they are thinking of someone and maybe start a conversation.

And this is why it is so helpful to have a 'persona' in mind for your content. A persona is essentially a fictional character who will play the role of your 'ideal audience'. In addition, the quickest and best way to find this persona is to think of people you know in your life. Write your content for them and make it so perfectly tailored for them and their ilk, that if you saw it you would just have to tag them in it, or post it to their wall.

An example of such tailored content might be an article about people who cannot concentrate when they are working from home – this would be perfect for us to share with someone works from home and whom we have maybe accused of slacking in the past. Likewise, a post on the return of a popular old band will likely get shared on the walls of people who are known for enjoying the music of that group.

Similarly, we post content like this on our own walls or like it as a way to communicate our interests and our lifestyles. When we like a post about a band that is our way of associating ourselves with that music and thereby expressing ourselves as individuals. Likewise, you may like or share an article on travelling if you think that is an important part of who you are (or if you want people to think, it is...).

In short, content that is well targeted at a specific audience will almost always perform particularly well in terms of shares and comments.

Oh and one more thing – people will often share or like content before they have even read it. This tells you right away how important it is to have a descriptive title and to pick the right image. Often people will like a post because they like the image – regardless of what the post is about!

Making Money and Generating Leads From Other People's Content

Finally, note that you can still also share the content of others through your page as long as it is relevant to your niche or industry. Ideally, this means sharing industry news and opinion pieces relating to your topic.

While this will mean sending people away from your brand, curating content is a service unto itself and you can still provide value this way. What's more, this lets you keep your page active without having to do anything yourself. Finally, it means that you can find content that has already been proven to be very successful and then benefit off the back of that.

Apps like Buzz Sumo (www.buzzsumo.com) make this very easy by letting you share popular content to your social accounts at the press of a button.

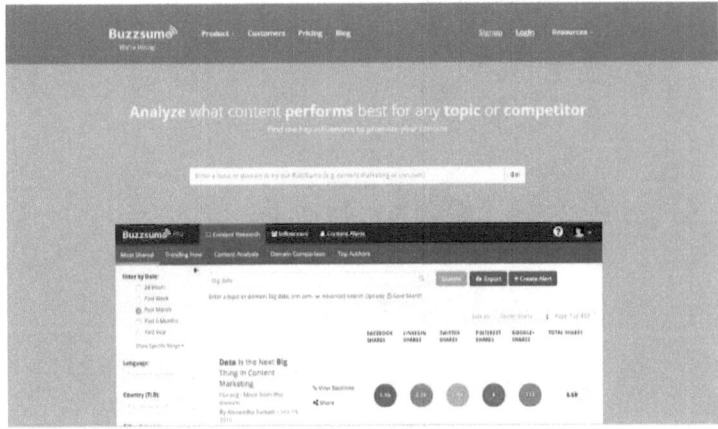

For advanced marketers, it is even possible to use some pop-up plugins to add e-mail opt-in forms to external content. By using a special link, you can send someone to third party content and then have a pop-up appear with your e-mail when they try to exit that page!

Chapter 6

Instagram

Instagram is now officially the second biggest social network behind Facebook. That is right; it is officially bigger than Twitter! Despite this, many companies are still not using this amazing tool to its fullest potential, read on to make sure you're not making the same mistake!

How Instagram Works

Like the other social networks, we have looked at, Instagram works in a unique way and has a unique set of features and uses.

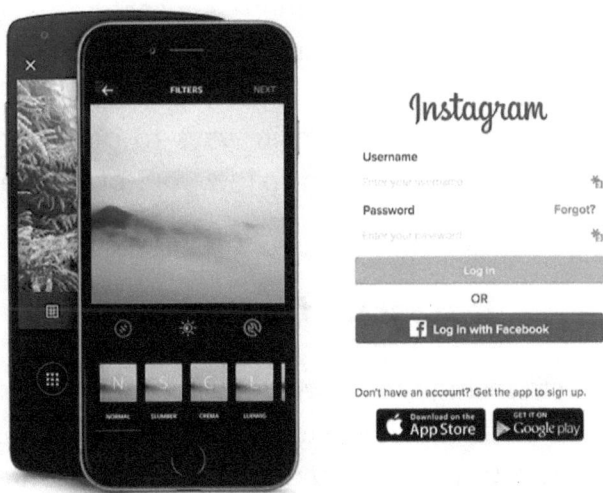

Essentially, Instagram is a photo sharing app. Unlike Facebook though (which now owns Instagram), the idea here is 'quality over quantity'. In other words, users do not upload their entire albums, but instead upload a few arty shots from their holidays or from little moments in their daily lives. When they do so, they will be given the opportunity to apply a number of different filters to further improve the appearance of their image and they can then write a comment complete with Twitter-style hashtags.

As with Twitter, users can then search for content by hashtag. Therefore, if you are on holiday in Paris, you might take a photo and tag it as '#Paris' and then click that tag to see all the other pictures that different users have uploaded of the city. You can also tag other users in your Instagram pictures – as with Facebook – and you can like the pictures that you see.

Like other social networks, you see pictures from the people you are following in your home feed. Unlike other social networks though, you do not also see content here that our contacts have liked. That said, there is a section to see photos that are 'popular in your network'.

Either way, in Instagram the main ways to get people to see your content are to have them follow you, or to use the right hashtags.

Instagram for Business

Like Pinterest, Instagram is very well suited to particularly 'visual' businesses. If you make clothes, or cakes, or you sell holidays, then you will have no difficulty finding content.

Again though, for everyone else, the secret is to look at the lifestyle behind your business and your niche. This might mean you're adding pictures of people working out again, or it might mean images of inspirational small businesses. Either way, you want your images to sell your value proposition in artistic and attractive ways.

As with Twitter, Instagram can also provide a handy way for people to get some insight into your business and to better understand how you operate. This means you might like to upload a picture of your office, or perhaps of your desk. You can get followers excited for an upcoming YouTube video for instance by showing a screenshot of your editing process, or of your camera and lighting set-up.

Though Facebook owns Instagram, it still has a little more synergy with Twitter and the two work very well together.

You can choose to share your Instagram posts to Twitter and when you do, they will have the same text and a link to the image. This is a good way to cross pollinate your Twitter and Instagram audiences and to conveniently add a visual element to your Twitter account. The other great thing about Instagram and Twitter alike is that you can quickly upload a photo or a post in minutes on your mobile phone and thereby ensure a stream of new content.

For your hashtags, you want to choose things that relate to your niche of course. At the same time, the objective should be to use things that lots of people will be looking for, but that won't have that much content yet.

So #sunset might be a bad choice because there are millions of photos with that hashtag and you will be drowned almost instantly in content. On the other hand, though, something like #twilight or #goldenlight might well get a lot of searches but not disappear quite so quickly.

Finally, note that you can use Instagram as a great way to run promotions and events and even to network in real life. For instance, if you run a high-street store, then why not get your customers to pose in your shop for a photo and then tag them in it?

There is a good chance that they will follow you in return! If you're at a networking event for marketers or bloggers meanwhile, then you could find someone there who is a big influencer then get a photo with them to upload and tag you both in – this could lead to exposure to a large audience!

Chapter 7

LinkedIn

We have discussed a bit about influencer marketing over the past several chapters but when it comes to this type of promotion, there is no platform better than LinkedIn.

Unlike other social networks that are designed for a commercial audience first and foremost, LinkedIn is built for businesses and as such contains many powerful tools that make it easier for you to promote yourself.

How LinkedIn Works for Businesses

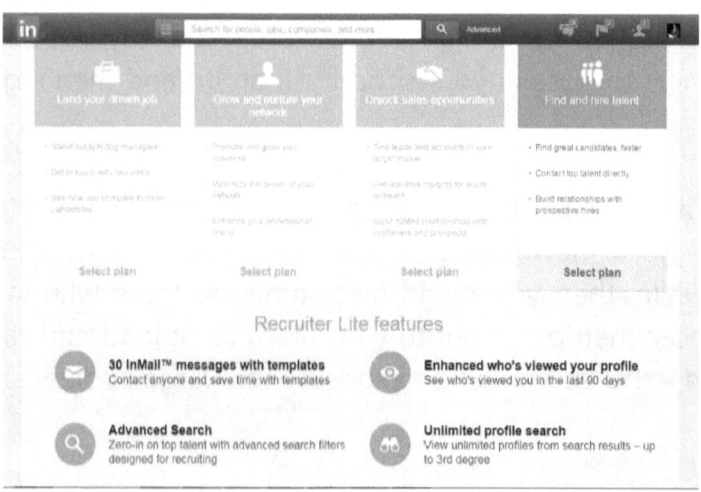

Standard LinkedIn profiles are for professionals to promote and network themselves. These work almost like CVs and allow people to show off their skills, often to try and find employment or clients. If you are a business then, you will need to set up a company page. Like a Facebook page, this can be accessed and managed from your main account but will have your company's branding instead of your picture.

Where the company page is slightly different from a Facebook page though, is in the inclusion of 'Showcase Pages', which were previously known as 'Products and Services' pages. The idea of a showcase page is essentially for you to show off the various things that your business has to offer. Therefore, if you have a website, then this is where you would put that.

This is an important distinction because the trading name of your business and the name of your website might be different. This also allows you to have and promote multiple different brands all at once. Microsoft for instance could set up a 'Microsoft' company page and then have showcase pages for 'Windows', 'Xbox', 'Microsoft Band', 'Surface' etc.

Because LinkedIn is all about professional networks, it is very useful for B2B businesses and you can even get direct sales this way.

Additional features of LinkedIn include 'Company Updates' which allow you to write posts from your business (rather than from yourself personally) and 'targeted company updates' which let you make posts that will be seen specifically by certain cross sections of your audience – for instance you might make a post that you want to be seen by the key decision makers of companies. You can also use this to discuss internal matters with the rest of your company and it's generally a great feature all around.

Additional Tricks and Features for Businesses

LinkedIn has a lot more tricks and features up its sleeve that are great for businesses and entrepreneurs. One particularly handy feature is the ability to look at other users and then to see how you might be connected. If you are not already connected to someone, then you may find that you are two degrees of separation away – which means you can now arrange an introduction. What's more, you can also use something called 'InMail' to message people who are somehow connected to you. Finally, the ability to see who the key 'influencers' are in your network is also very useful.

LinkedIn is very powerful, when you use it to make connections and to find other businesses and bloggers to work with. Look up a big name blogger in your niche and you might find that you know someone who knows them and can arrange and introduction. From there, you can then look into working together to promote both your businesses.

LinkedIn is generally a great tool for networking. If you attend networking events (and you should) you can also use it to turn those chance encounters into lasting contacts. Two tools that can help you to do this are Rapportive (www.razosocial.com/linkedin-tools/) and FiveHundredPlus (www.fivehundredplus.com).

Rapportive is an excellent plugin for Gmail that allows you to see the LinkedIn profile of anyone who e-mails you. This way, someone who you are dealing with for the first time can now become a long-term contact and you'll be able to potentially benefit from their connections too. This also means that you will know precisely who is messaging you (which is very useful) and it means that you can turn any business card you are given into a new LinkedIn connection.

Note that you can also use LinkedIn just like Facebook or Twitter but with a more targeted B2B audience. It's easy to share posts, status updates, photos and more on LinkedIn and you can even try using 'LinkedIn Pulse' which is essentially an in-built blogging platform for industry news.

Chapter 8
Google+

Google+ is the newest kid on the block, though it has been around for a while now and is clearly here to stay. And like blogging, it seems like this is an area of particular interest for many marketers and businesses going forward. Social Media Examiner found that of all the social networks, Google+ was the one that people were most interested in learning about. 54% of marketers are already using it and 61% plan on increasing their G+ activities.

The Unique Benefits of Google+

Largely what makes Google+ popular is the way it ties into SEO as well as providing the usual social media marketing benefits. Of course, G+ is owned by Google, which means that it has been integrated with the search engine algorithms. Getting '+1s' on this network can help your content appear in personalized search and may even contribute to overall rankings according to MOZ.

What's more, Google+ has a useful 'Hangouts' feature for live chat in groups, it integrates well with Gmail and it has a good community's tool. Google+ is interesting at the moment, for while it hasn't seen quite the widespread adoption as Facebook or Twitter, its links with Google mean it's very popular among marketers and bloggers. This in turn means that like LinkedIn, it is a good place for marketers to network.

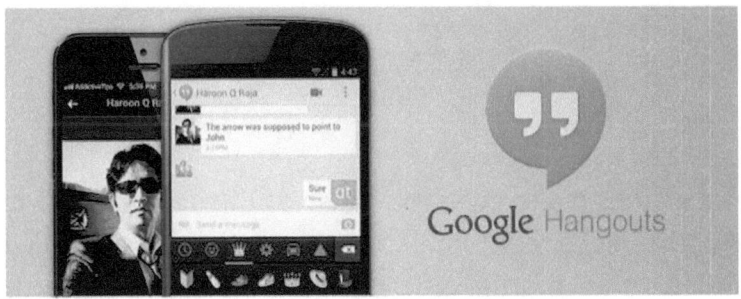

Tips to Succeed on Google+

When it comes to sharing content, the same rules apply for Google+ as for Facebook. However, it is well worth joining some of the communities on the site which range from just about every niche imaginable.

You can then post in these communities and your content will be seen by a large number of the members right on their home feeds. This is a very quick way to not only build a lot of +1s but to potentially generate a huge amount of direct traffic. It is actually very similar to a site like Reddit in this case – almost like social bookmarking.

A smart way to make even more use of this feature is to create some cross-niche content. For instance, write an article on bodybuilding for martial artists and that way you can promote your weight loss supplement to a new audience. Style for bloggers? Top books to enjoy while fishing? There are plenty of possibilities here and again this works very well on Reddit.

To build your circles (which is the G+ equivalent of followers), you can also take part in discussions in these communities and in hangouts. This lets you demonstrate your authority on a subject and make contacts. Another simple strategy is to add more people to your own circles – they will be notified and will very often respond in kind.

Finally, make sure to officially link your G+ page with your website so that Google sees you as the author. This may have more SEO benefit.

Chapter 10

Live Video Streaming

When it comes to video marketing, the next evolution it seems is going to be live video streaming. Live streaming has been available through YouTube for a while now but it is only recently that channels have started taking advantage of this more regularly. This way, they can stream events, Q&As or other live events. Live gaming has also been popular for a while thanks to Twitch, which now has 45 million monthly viewers (www.twitch.com).

Live video has a special appeal for viewers because it is happening now. Not only does this mean it is often available only for a limited time (unless it is recorded and uploaded) but also it means that they can be the first to learn of certain events. More than pre-recorded video, live events can transport the viewers to somewhere new and indeed the tagline for Periscope is 'Explore the World through Someone Else's Eyes'.

Apps for Live Streaming

What really jumpstarted the popularity of video streaming though are Periscope (www.periscope.com) and Meerkat (www.meerkatapp.co).

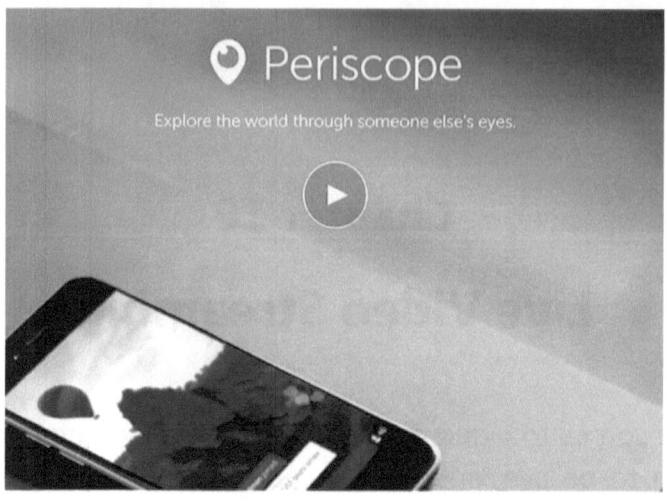

These are two streaming apps, that let users broadcast their feeds and which have garnered a lot of attention, very quickly. Anyone can use Periscope and a number of brands are already using it to great effect. Red Bull for instance used Periscope recently to stream Guest House events, while Spotify posts things like behind-the-scenes videos with artists.

Other options for live streaming include Blab (www.blab.im), YouTube and even SnapChat (www.snapchat.com) to some extent.

Each can be used in a similar way to help generate buzz around a live event and to give your audience a live window through which they can view your business. If you are only going to focus on one though, choose either YouTube or Periscope. The latter is quickly growing in popularity to become the streaming service of choice for marketers and has a very positive buzz at the moment that you can benefit from.

Tips for Success

To succeed through live video, the secret is yet again to provide value as information and entertainment. However, at the same time, it has to use other social media platforms to generate hype and buzz for your event – start promoting your live streaming event early on and find ways to engage your audience by inviting them to participate in various ways where applicable.

This is also great for tying together with competitions and other types of time-sensitive marketing. Think too about things that benefit from being live – concerts, travel, interviews and more all feel a lot more exciting when live. How about a live launch event for your product? Likewise, how about letting your viewers send in live questions, something that can be exciting and give them direct access to your brand. Make sure that your audience feel as though they are getting live, unrestricted access to something exciting and different and you will be able to generate excitement.

And if you're not quite ready to go live in front of the camera yet, consider using other live 'events' for your marketing. This could mean a Reddit AMA (Ask Me Anything) or a Google Hangout.

Conclusion:

How Do You Want To Be Known On Social Media?

That is a lot of information we have covered and a lot of different strategies. We have seen how to set up a social media empire and how to thrive across all platforms and on certain platforms specifically. We have looked at how to leverage new emerging technologies, we have seen apps and tools you can use and we have addressed the psychology of sharing.

However, throughout all of this, what has remained the most important is that you deliver value. Value is what draws people to any social media account, just as it is what draws them to a website. Value is what keeps them there and it is what keeps them clicking on your links and sharing your posts.

Moreover, value is what helps you to build your reputation as a brand that can deliver. And this is absolutely crucial – because there's no point having a big audience if that audience doesn't trust you and isn't interested in what you have to offer. Do not post clickbait or spam the web with promotional messages – use your social media accounts to show what is important to your organization, to entertain your visitors and to show that you know your topic inside out.

Likewise, make sure that you are actually engaging with the audience that visit your site. Respond to comments, ask questions and contribute to the communities you join. This way people will feel like they know you and they will go from being customers and leads to being fans and real contacts. Every single one of those followers can be turned into a fan and 1,000 true fans is really all any business needs to go nuclear.

The key then is truly to just think carefully about what you post and to hold yourself to high standards. Think about how you want to be seen on social media and about what impression you want to make. If you do this, then you will find that you attract new followers and new customers like a magnet.

Social media is like a megaphone that will amplify your message. This can be irritating, or it can be a great way to demonstrate your enthusiasm and passion to the masses.

David Odunaiya & Abiola Fashina Esq.

ABOUT THE AUTHORS

David Odunaiya

David Odunaiya was born in England, UK in 1966. He is an ordained Bible Teacher and has taught in Churches, Bible Schools and in the Mission field for over 20 years. He is also an author, conference speaker, business coach, online entrepreneur and publisher.

He is the President of David Odunaiya Ministries International [DOMI} and the CEO of GLOBAL NETWORK PUBLISHING HOUSE with headquarters in Liverpool, United Kingdom. As a publisher, he has a vision to bridge the gap between Christian authors in less developed countries and the western world. With this vision in mind, he has dedicated himself to empowering other aspiring authors in the body of Christians with the knowledge and experience to become successful self-published authors.

He has authored books such as;

- The pain and the passion of Christ
- The mystery of the holy communion
- When I see the blood
- 10 ways your dream with your life
- and many more

All books are available on www.amazon.co.uk

He provides coaching advice/tips through his podcasts, website, newsletters and books. He holds online training/courses to provide Training/Coaching for aspiring authors.

Author details:

Website: www.davidoduniya.com
Email: info@davidodunaiya.com
Telephone: +447878484162

Office: Liverpool, United Kingdom

Abiola Fashina Esq.

 Abiola Fashina Esq. is the CEO of the Atlanta Georgia USA based nonprofit organization, magazine MyFaithTV Network International Inc.

A lawyer, business, entrepreneur, magazine and book publisher, international marketing & social media consultant and international conference convener & facilitator. Abiola Fashina Esq. has for several years trained entrepreneurs, small business owners, churches, companies, corporate outfits and nonprofit organizations on how to use social media to attract more customers, increase sales & ROI and expand their organizations globally.

Every year, Abiola Fashina Esq. host several **GLOBAL LEADERSHIP & MEDIA EMPOWERMENT CONFERENCES**, trainings and workshops nationally in the USA and also in different continents all over the world (GO GLOBAL CONFERENCES. www.goglobalconferences.org).

The mission of the **GOGLOBAL CONFERENCES**, trainings and workshops are to disseminate information and to train participants on how to utilize technology and social media for global expansion. These conferences, trainings and workshops are attended by thousands of representatives of small businesses organizations, companies, Churches and ministries as well as by authors, music artists and entertainment industry practitioners, corporate leaders. Pastors, Ministers and nonprofit organization operators in attendance.

Author details:

Website: www.myfaithtvnetwork.com
www.goglobalconferences.org
Email: info@myfaithtvnetwork.com
Telephone: +1 678 886 5117

Office: Atlanta, Georgia, USA

www.ingramcontent.com/pod-product-compliance
Lightning Source LLC
Chambersburg PA
CBHW021351170526
45164CB00003B/363